COPYRIGHT 2022
BY NANCY DORT ROSSOW

ALL RIGHTS RESERVED. THIS BOOK OR
ANY PORTION THEREOF MAY NOT BE
REPRODUCED IN ANY MANNER
WHATSOEVER WITHOUT THE EXPRESS
WRITTEN PERMISSION OF THE COPYRIGHT
HOLDER EXCEPT FOR THE USE OF BRIEF
QUOTATIONS IN A REVIEW.

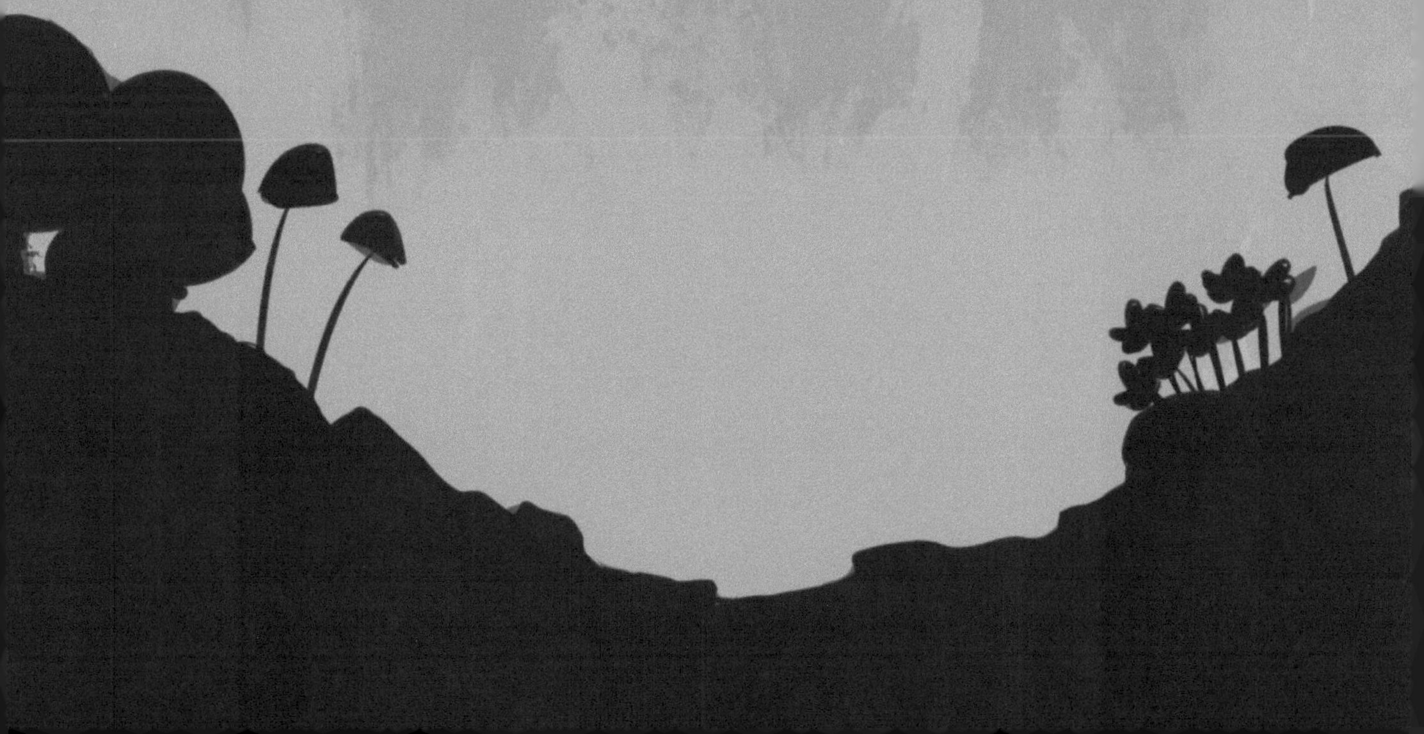

FOR MY FAMILY.
THANKS FOR ALL YOUR
ENCOURAGEMENT.

Rarely seen, except at night.
Using sonar in your flight.
Stealthy creature in the air,
Sneaking by us, unaware.

You are a:
BAT!

Floating on air, with stained glass wings.
One of Creation's most beautiful things.
Migrating south when the weather turns cold.
Fluttering art for the eye to behold.

You are a:
BUTTERFLY!

This lowly insect, I think you'd agree,
is one prehistoric pest.
Just turn on the light;
they'll scatter and flee,
and live longer than the rest.

You are a
COCKROACH!

You rub your wings together, and create a chirping sound,
that seems to come from here and there, and everywhere around.
And when the moon and stars come out, more chirping can be heard!
Why don't you sleep at nighttime, like some considerate bird?

You are a
CRICKET!

This gangly, delicate creature
looks funny when it walks.
It seems to just be balancing on
stilts or skinny stalks.
And if by chance you catch it, it
might leave a leg behind,
but since it grows another one,
it doesn't seem to mind.

You are a
DADDY LONG
LEGS!

This insect is the environment's friend,
it scoops up the dung from
a cattle's back end.
It rolls, and buries the poop in the ground,
Which helps the grass grow and the flowers
abound.

You are a
DUNG BEETLE!

From daisy to pansy, to clover and back,
You gather up pollen to put in your sac.
Without you the flowers might all fade away,
and we'd have no honey to sweeten our day.

You are a:
HONEYBEE!

You look like a crab with pincer-like claws.
Your tail is used to stun prey.
Instead of biting with your tiny jaws,
You sting and scurry away.

You are a
SCORPION!

Slow-moving, slithering, slimy — ugh!
You really are a strange looking bug.
You don't have a home
that you take on the trail,
no shell on your back like your
cousin the snail.

You are a
SLUG!

I saw a creature slithering,
then drop its skin along…
I do believe it's littering,
and don't you think that's wrong?

You are a
SNAKE!

You eat the plants in the
garden I've grown…
it's all that you know how to do.
So, please take your shell and leave me alone,
or I will make escargot stew.

You are a
SNAIL!

Insects have six,
and you have eight,
not eyes, not wings,
but legs.
You spin a web and
set the bait,
catch prey, and
lay your eggs.

You are a
SPIDER!

You're similar to a frog;
often found in a swampy bog;
while living under a log.
You croak if you're in the mood;
and a poison you may exude;
bugs are your favorite food.

You are a
TOAD!

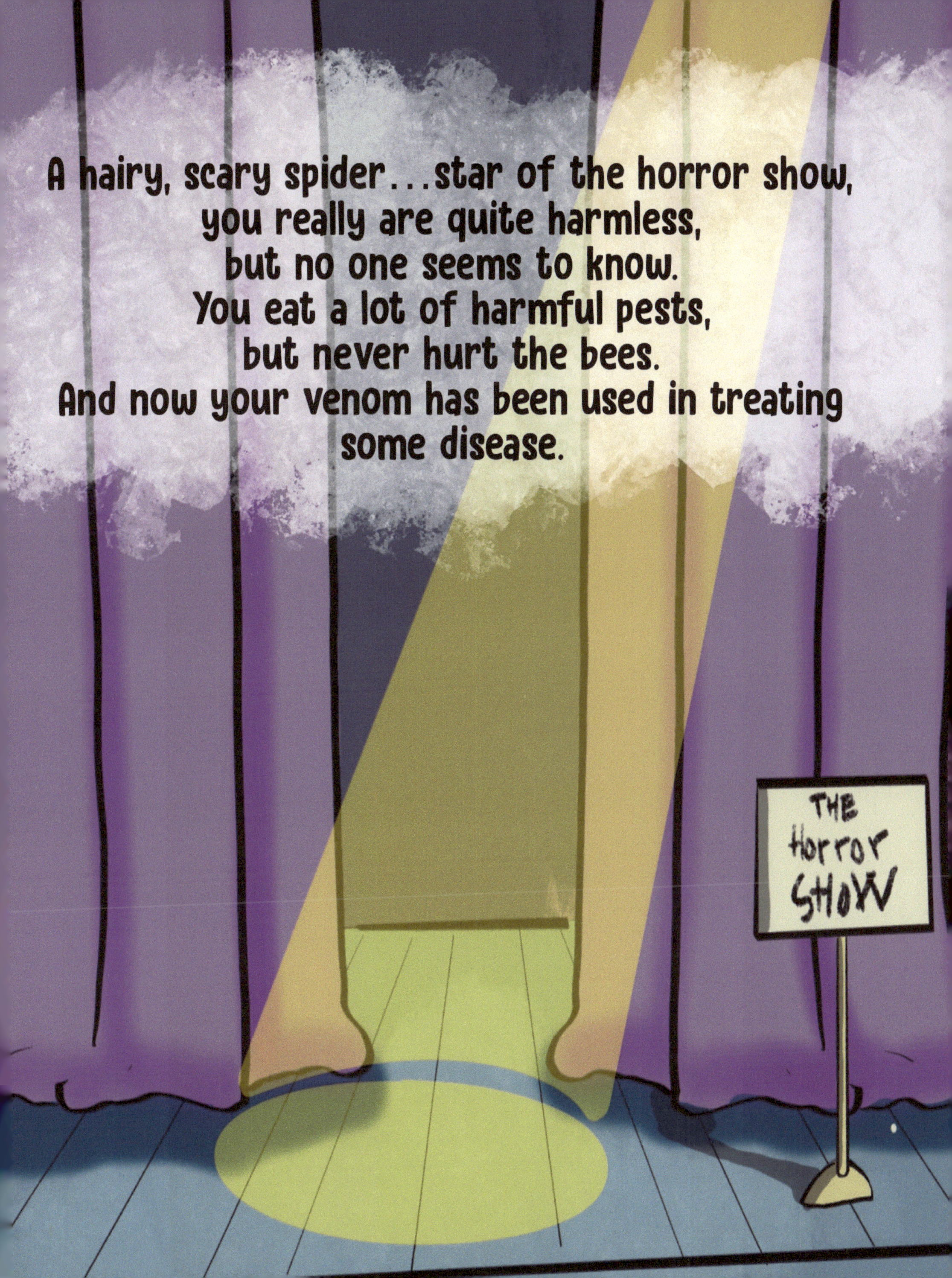

A hairy, scary spider...star of the horror show,
you really are quite harmless,
but no one seems to know.
You eat a lot of harmful pests,
but never hurt the bees.
And now your venom has been used in treating
some disease.

THE
Horror
SHOW

You are a
TARANTULA!
THE
Horror
SHOW

ABOUT THE AUTHOR
NANCY DORT ROSSOW, PH.D

IS A RETIRED SCHOOL
PSYCHOLOGIST AND UNIVERSITY INSTRUCTOR. SHE WAS A FORMER
BIOLOGY TEACHER, AND CURRENTLY WRITES NOVELS AND PICTURE
BOOKS. SHE IS THE MOTHER OF TWO GROWN WOMEN AND SPLITS HER
TIME BETWEEN FLORIDA AND COLORADO. HER DEBUT NOVEL,
A DEEP PLACE OF GRACE, IS AVAILABLE IN

YOUNG BOOKWORMS GIFT AND BOOKSTORE, AND
ONLINE AT AMAZON.COM, AND YOUNGBOOKWORMS.COM.

ABOUT THE ARTIST

I LOVE TO CREATE, WHETHER IT IS OUT OF MY OWN
IMAGINATION OR THE IMAGINATION OF OTHERS. NOTHING
BRINGS ME MORE JOY THAN TO SIT IN FRONT OF AN
EMPTY PAGE AND START TO MAKE IDEAS A REALITY!

I HAVE BEEN ILLUSTRATING SINCE I CAN REMEMBER. WHETHER IT'S
CHILDRENS BOOKS, GRAPHIC NOVELS, BOARD GAMES, OR MOVIE SETS, I
LOVE EVERY ASPECT OF CREATING SOMETHING NEW.

WWW.JUSTINDUNNILLUSTRATIONS.SQUARESPACE.COM

www.ingramcontent.com/pod-product-compliance
Lightning Source LLC
Chambersburg PA
CBHW040210240726
48664CB00002B/898